Home Safety

BY SUSAN KESSELRING   childsworld.com   ILLUSTRATED BY DAN McGEEHAN

Published by The Child's World®
800-599-READ • childsworld.com

Copyright © 2025 by The Child's World®
All rights reserved. No part of this book may be reproduced or utilized in any form or by any means without written permission from the publisher.

ISBN Information
9781503893979 (Reinforced Library Binding)
9781503895072 (Portable Document Format)
9781503895898 (Online Multi-user eBook)
9781503896710 (Electronic Publication)

LCCN
2024942719

Printed in the United States of America

ABOUT THE AUTHOR
Susan Kesselring loves children, books, nature, and her family. She teaches K-1 students in a progressive charter school down a little country lane in Castle Rock, Minnesota. She is the mother of five daughters and lives in Apple Valley, Minnesota with her husband and a crazy springer spaniel named Lois Lane.

ABOUT THE ILLUSTRATOR
Dan McGeehan spent his younger years as an actor, author, playwright, and editor. Now he spends his days drawing, and he is much happier.

TABLE OF CONTENTS

CHAPTER ONE
Safety At Home . . . 4

CHAPTER TWO
In the Kitchen . . . 7

CHAPTER THREE
Stepping, Skipping, and Climbing . . . 8

CHAPTER FOUR
Choking . . . 11

CHAPTER FIVE
Fire Safety . . . 12

CHAPTER SIX
Poisons . . . 15

CHAPTER SEVEN
Not for Kids . . . 16

CHAPTER EIGHT
Calling 911 . . . 19

Home Safety Rules . . . 20
Wonder More . . . 21
Home Safety Hunt . . . 22
Glossary . . . 23
Find Out More . . . 24
Index . . . 24

CHAPTER 1

Safety At Home

What fun things do you do at home? Are you a block builder or a car racer? Do you dress up dolls or put puzzles together? Or do you like to make popcorn or grilled-cheese sandwiches with your parents?

Hi! I'm Buzz B. Safe. Watch for me! I'll show you how to be safe at home.

Puzzles and board games can be safe activities for everyone.

Playing and cooking at home can be fun! You do have to be careful, though. Just remember to follow a few safety rules and you won't get hurt.

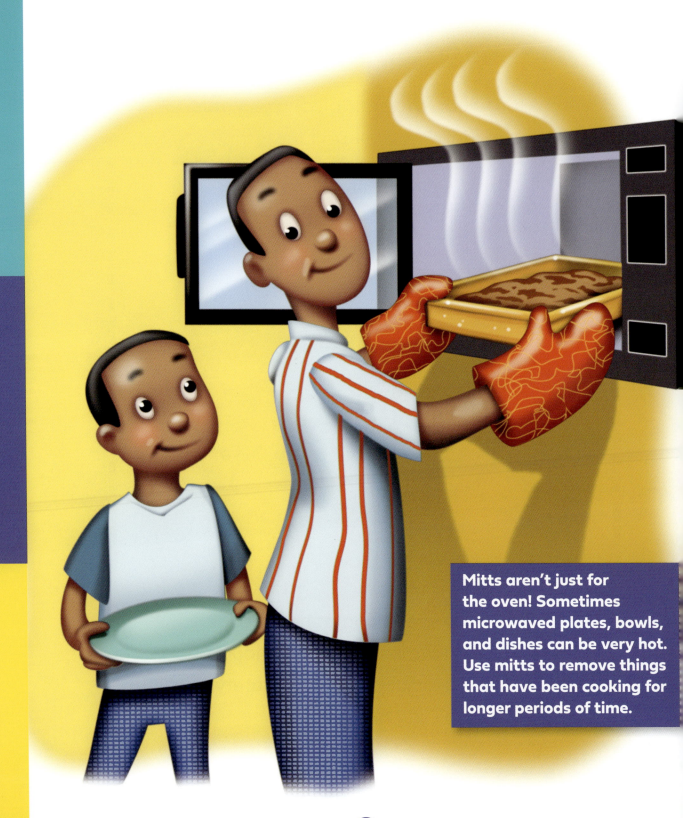

Mitts aren't just for the oven! Sometimes microwaved plates, bowls, and dishes can be very hot. Use mitts to remove things that have been cooking for longer periods of time.

CHAPTER 2

In the Kitchen

Cooking is a yummy way to have fun! But be careful with hot food. Always ask an adult to take the hot food out of a microwave or an oven for you.

It is easy to cut yourself with a sharp knife. Let your parent chop the vegetables and slice the bread.

Even though you can't use a knife, you can still help out at dinnertime. Offer to wash the vegetables or set the table.

CHAPTER 3

Stepping, Skipping, and Climbing

It's great to move, skip, and dance in your home. You could trip or fall if you do not have a clear path, though. Pick up toys and keep other things off the stairs and floors. You don't want anyone else to fall, either.

Watch where you step in the bathroom or the kitchen. Water may have trickled on the floor. It could be slippery.

Keeping your toys picked up also keeps them from getting lost or broken!

Climbing on play equipment outside is a terrific way to play. But when you're inside, climbing is not safe. Stay off tall furniture, drawers, and shelves. They could fall onto you.

Window screens keep bugs out of your home. They are not very strong, though. They will not keep you from falling out. It's safest to play away from open windows.

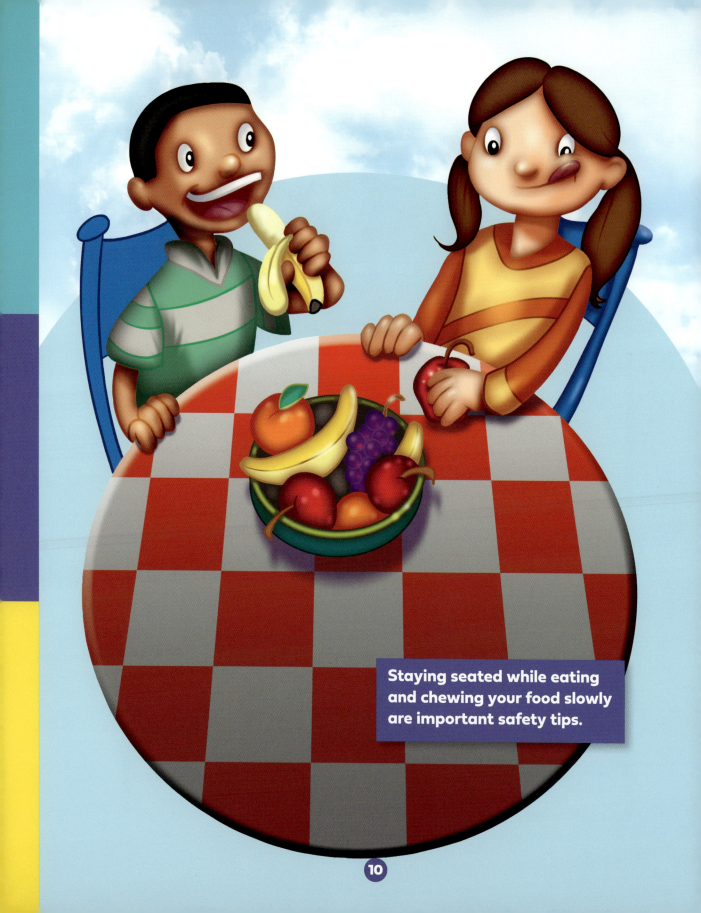

CHAPTER 4

Choking

Always stay sitting at the table when you eat. Chew your food slowly and completely. Also, keep small objects out of your mouth. Toys, coins, balls, and balloons are not supposed to be chewed.

Keep plastic away from your head and face. Plastic covering your nose or mouth can make it hard for you to breathe.

Be careful around drapes and blinds. Their cords could twist around your neck and choke you.

CHAPTER 5

Fire Safety

A fire in the fireplace is warm and cozy. But a fire in your home is dangerous. Make a plan with your family for how to escape your home if there is a fire. Choose a spot outside where you will all meet. Practice your plan. Then you'll know what to do in a real fire.

Smoke detectors "smell" smoke before you can. Their loud alarms tell you there is a fire. You should have one on every floor of your home and near bedrooms.

Only cords should be plugged into wall **sockets**. If toys or other objects are stuck into wall sockets, you could get an electric **shock**.

Electricity moves quickly through water. If hair dryers and other things that are plugged in fall into water, they can give you an electric shock. Keep them away from sinks or tubs.

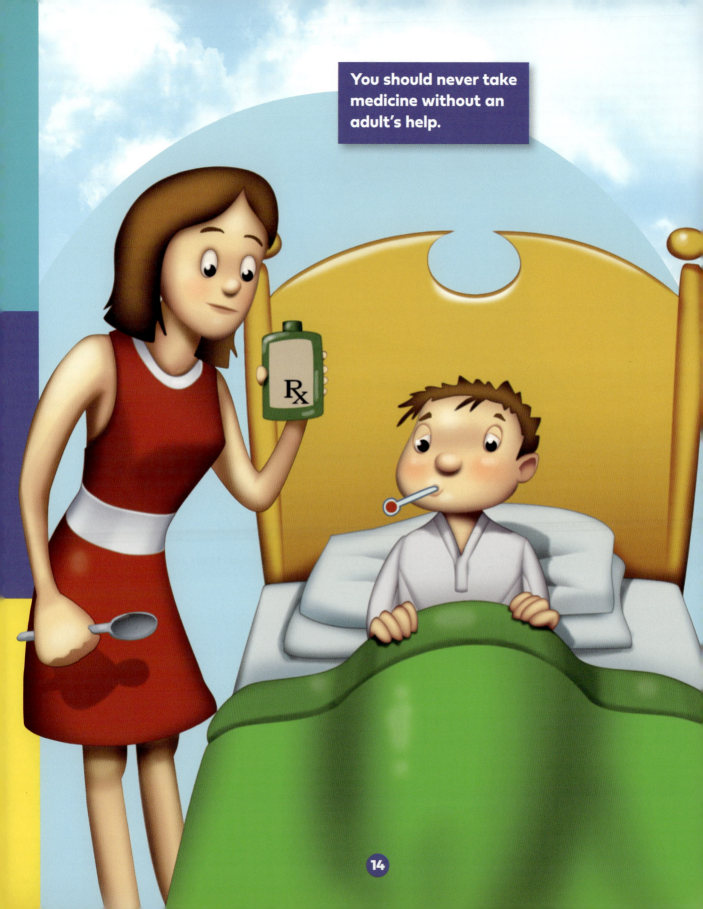

CHAPTER 6

Poisons

Many things used in your home are **poisons**. Cleaning products should only be used for cleaning. Ask an adult before you eat or drink anything you aren't sure about.

Some medicine looks like candy. But medicine can make you very sick if it's not yours. Even when it's your own medicine, be sure to ask an adult for help.

If a poison accidentally gets in your mouth, tell a parent right away. He or she will call a poison control center or 911 to get you help.

CHAPTER 7

Not for Kids

Some things at home are not for children. If you find matches or lighters, tell an adult right away. He or she can put them up high so no one gets hurt.

Do your parents have guns at home? Guns should always be locked up. If you see a gun lying around, never touch it. Run and tell an adult as fast as you can.

Guns should never be played with. They are not toys!

If you call 911, don't hang up right away. The person may tell you instructions about what to do.

Chapter 8
Calling 911

Do you know what to do if there is an emergency at home? Call 911. Explain the problem to the person on the phone. Sometimes he or she can tell where your call is coming from. But you may need to give the person your address. Knowing it will save precious time. Help will be sent to your house.

Learning these safety rules will keep you and your family safe at home.

Home Safety Rules

- Let an adult help you with hot foods and sharp knives.
- Keep toys and other things off floors so no one trips.
- Sit down when you are eating.
- Keep objects that are not food out of your mouth.
- Practice a plan for getting out of your home if there is a fire.
- Tell an adult if you find matches, lighters, or guns.
- Ask an adult before you eat or drink anything that is not obviously food.
- Call 911 if there is an emergency at home.

Always be safe!

Wonder More

Wondering about New Information

How much did you know about home safety before you read this book? What new information did you learn? Write down three new facts that this book taught you. Was the new information surprising? Why or why not?

Wondering How It Matters

Do you know anyone who had an accident or got hurt at home? What could have been done to prevent it?

Wondering Why

Why is it important to have rules about safety in your home? What do you think might happen if you didn't act safely in your home?

Ways to Keep Wondering

After reading this book, what questions do you have about home safety? What can you do to learn more about it?

Home Safety Hunt

Search for safety—and dangers—in your home.

You will need:
- A marker, pen, or pencil
- A list of safety items on a piece of paper. Some ideas:
  - a smoke detector
  - a fire extinguisher
  - electrical outlets with covers
  - sharp items (scissors or knives) not put away
  - toys not put away

Instructions:
Take your list and a marker, pen, or pencil and walk around your home. See how many things you can check off your safety list. If you see dangerous items, tell an adult right away!

Home Safety Hunt
- ☐ smoke detector
- ☐ fire extinguisher
- ☐ covered electrical outlet
- ☐ sharp item not put away
- ☐ toy not put away

Glossary

poisons (POY-zuns): Poisons are substances that can harm or kill someone if put in the body. Some cleaning products are poisons.

shock (SHOK): A shock is the passing of electricity through someone's body. A hair dryer that touches water can cause a hurtful shock.

smoke detectors (SMOHK di-TEK-turs): Smoke detectors are devices that make loud noises to tell you there is smoke. Smoke detectors can warn you of a fire.

sockets (SOK-its): Sockets are the places in walls where you plug in electric cords. Do not put anything other than plugs in sockets.

Find Out More

In the Library

Bellisario, Gina. *Poison Alert!: My Tips to Avoid Danger Zones at Home*. Minneapolis, MN: Millbrook Press, 2014.

Emminizer, Theresa. *Saying Safe at Home*. Buffalo, NY: PowerKids Press, 2024.

Hodge, Krystle. *SafetyKay's Home Adventures: Child Home Safety Book*. Independently Published, 2024.

On the Web

Visit our Web site for links about home safety:
childsworld.com/links

Note to Parents, Teachers, and Librarians: We routinely verify our Web links to make sure they are safe and active sites. So encourage your readers to check them out!

Index

911, 15, 18, 19
cooking, 5, 7
choking, 11
climbing, 8, 9
drapes, 11
eating, 10, 11, 15
electricity, 13
fire, 12

gun, 16
knife, 7
lighter, 16, 17
matches, 16
medicine, 14, 15
microwave, 6
mitt, 6
oven, 6, 7

shock, 13
smoke, 12
stairs, 8
toys, 8, 9, 11, 13, 16
water, 8, 13
windows, 9